Presented to:

_____

From:

_____

D. C. GOMEZ

DARE TO FORGIVE

A 4 Week Devotional to help you heal the wounds of the past by forgiving yourself and others.

BY D. C GOMEZ

D. C. GOMEZ

Dare to Forgive
ISBN: 978-1-7333160-6-4 (paperback)
Published by Gomez Expeditions
Request to publish work from this book should be sent to:
author@dcgomez-author.com

I dedicate the *Dare Collection* to my parents:

Two of the most passionate people I have ever met.
They embrace life to the fullest. When life was full of
challenges and difficulties, they focused on the positive side
of things and finding humor in everything. Every adventure I
have undertaken, they have been my greatest cheerleaders.

Thank you for loving life and sharing it
with everyone you meet.

D. C. GOMEZ

INTRODUCTION

When the Lord whispered the idea for the Dare Collection to me, I was overwhelmed, terrified, and didn't feel qualified to take this on. I had other things I had planned to work on. A devotional was not something I had planned for. But like many of his plans for us, the results are better than anything I ever expected. After putting my fears aside, I embarked on this journey. I'm excited to bring you book two in the Dare Collection: Dare to Forgive.

Many things in my life changed when I decided I wanted to be happy. For years I had been weighed down by shame, guilt, insecurities, and resentments. I was angry at myself, and even members of my family for things that had happened years ago. I couldn't figure out why I wasn't able to feel at peace with myself, or have healthy, happy relationships. It wasn't until I committed to my self-discovery and healing that I found out the anger, hate, and bitterness I was feeling had become a permanent companion in my life.

It was almost impossible for positive, healthy emotions to take root in my heart for long periods of time when I was filled with so much poison. Before I could make my dreams come true, I needed to cleanse and heal my soul. The process was scary. I had to face my own demons and accept myself with all of my flaws and insecurities instead of hiding behind a mask. After years of pushing the real me away, I had to learn to love that person again. To truly believe that person was worthy of being forgiven, loved, and cared for.

If your relationships are feeling stale, or you're having a hard time moving forward in life, I challenge you to take some time to reflect on your life. Are you holding grudges against others? Are you harboring ill feelings toward yourself and those around you? It's hard for our lives to move forward when we're stuck in one area. By learning to forgive, you will unblock the energy that is holding you back. It will give you an opportunity to bring peace to your life and not be moved by the whims of others.

I would like to thank you for taking the time and for investing in this devotional. As we embark on this four-week journey together, you will discover the devotional is broken down into four weeks. The first week we will focus on looking at how anger is holding us back. In week two, we will focus on forgiving others. Week three is where we will face our own self guilt and hatred so we can work on forgiving ourselves. For week four, we will bring it all together by focusing on living a life of peace by not holding anger, bitterness, or resentment in our hearts.

Each day we are starting with a scripture, followed by an inspirational moment. I recommend you take some time each day to do your own reflection as part of your own journey. You will have space at the end of each day to write your own experiences. We will grow in this journey together to dare to forgive, to know we are worthy of a beautiful future. My prayer for you, my friend, is that you live your best life now.

DARE TO FORGIVE

9

WHAT HOLDS US BACK?

Forgiveness is something we all struggle with. Many of us have experienced painful events in our lives. Some things we had no control over; things that were done to us by people we loved or trusted. How do we let go years of anger, pain, trauma, and suffering? We must first realize how the pain is affecting us before we can decide to do something about it.

Anger is a normal human emotion. While it is normal, it's not healthy living in that state filled with constant resentment. The problem is it feels good to be angry. The rush we get feeds our egos. We enjoy the sense of getting vengeance and defending who we are. But according to Eckhart Tolle, "the truth needs no defending." This week we are going to explore what the scriptures say about anger and how it's holding us back.

DAY 1

"For the stirring of milk brings forth curds, and the stirring of anger brings forth blood." (Proverbs 30:33)

Every action has an equal and opposite reaction. This is one law we learned in high school. What most teachers fail to explain is that this applies to every area of our lives. Every action we do, or others do, has a consequence. It might not be visible immediately, but the aftermath has an effect in our lives.

Anger is a natural human response. For many of us, it stirs us into action. The question is, are those actions for the good or evil of ourselves and others? How we channel that energy will determine the results we get from it. If the intentions behind our anger is to pay others back, hate will continue to spread. As the scripture above says, when we make decisions based on our anger, people will get hurt and blood will follow.

If we can get past our feelings and not react out of hate, we can break the cycle. We might not control what others do, or even how they treat us, but we can control our reaction to the situation. We have the power to determine how long we allow the anger to control us and when we take our lives back.

Reflection Time

When you're upset or overwhelmed, how long does it take you to calm down? Do you find it difficult to relax after an altercation?

_____

_____

_____

_____

_____

_____

_____

_____

_____

_____

_____

_____

DAY 2

"Nay, impatience kills the fool and indignation slays the simpleton. I have seen a fool spreading his roots, but his household suddenly decayed."
(Job 5:2-3)

Have you met a person who has been holding on to an offense for years? They're still angry and upset over something that was done to them, and they are still indignant about it. They talk about the situation like it happened yesterday. All of their actions are based on what has happened to them, and it makes them afraid to experience the same thing again. Their resentment is so bad that they avoid the other person while talking bad about them to anyone they meet.

Some of us have met this individual. We have even been this individual allowing the pain others caused us to mask everything we do. But look at the scripture above, my friends. "… indignation slays the simpleton." Being upset, while it might make us feel validated and fill our souls with sympathy, it makes us do foolish things. We stop looking toward the future because we are too consumed with being angry that we're living in the past.

Do we really want our future to wash away because of the anger we're holding on to? If it's not serving you to be upset over a negative situation, then it's time to stop holding on to it. We have a choice to leave those feelings to the simpleton and rise above them. Our future is too great to allow our past to hold us back.

Reflection Time:

When anger hits you, what is your first reaction? Are you quick to jump to conclusions, attacking others, or are you able to take a step back and look at the entire picture? As you write these down, don't judge yourself, my friends. This exercise is to give you a starting point for you to know where you are in your life.

_____

_____

_____

_____

_____

_____

_____

_____

_____

_____

_____

DAY 3

"Say not, 'As he did to me, so will I do to him; I will repay the man according to his deeds.'" (Proverbs 24:29)

The Old Testament is full of statements like an eye for an eye and a tooth for a tooth. The origin behind that phrase is not one many people in current times know. This was never meant for individuals to act their vengeance upon others for wrongdoing. Back in the early beginnings of humanity, the world was a very different place, and it had no organized justice system. The idea behind it was to stop individuals from killing others for minor offenses. The theory was simple: the punishment has to match the crime. It's very similar to what we practice today.

As society progressed, systems provided order and justice to communities. Individuals are no longer acting like judges and enforcers for crimes, at least not in the legal sense of the word. Still, some of us are still focused on trying to pay people back for the things they've done to us by holding on to that old saying. Interestingly, as the scripture above states, even the Old Testament is asking individuals to stop that mind set. To quote the famous Gandhi, "An eye for an eye leaves the whole world blind."

Gandhi's perspective is refreshing. Trying to pay people back only creates more pain in the world and in our own lives. Anger feeds anger, and the results can be destructive. Don't focus your energy, my friends, on repaying others. Instead, channel it to make yourself happy. Time is very limited, so take full advantage of it.

Reflection Time:

Have you ever tried to pay someone back for something they did to you? How did it feel? Did you truly receive the peace and compensation you were looking for?

_____

_____

_____

_____

_____

_____

_____

_____

_____

_____

_____

_____

DAY 4

"Do not in spirit become quickly discontent, for discontent lodges in the bosom of a fool." (Ecclesiastes 7:9)

I used to believe that I was not a patient person, and I used this as an excuse to become easily frustrated. For years I was annoyed because things weren't happening on my timetable. I would become judgmental of those around me when they weren't doing the things I thought were important. Those feelings started taking root in my soul and clouding the way I saw the world and the people around me.

It took me a while to realize that patience was a choice. I was choosing to become quickly annoyed by the actions of others and things outside of my control. Ecclesiastes is challenging us to not allow these emotions to take control of our lives and ruin our days. While my anger came quickly, it did not leave at the same speed. It lingered, making me prickly and hard to deal with. As a result, I became more irritated about how people were treating me. This became a vicious cycle.

The choice was mine, and it gave me a sense of power and security. By not allowing the anger and judgement to take hold from the beginning, I could discern the situation more carefully. With a sense of separation, I could analyze things without getting my feelings hurt. This all started by choosing not to react quickly to everything that happened to me.

Reflection Time:

Have you had a situation where you were the calming voice in the room? Where you were the one who was able to provide clarity to all the people involved? How did you handle it, and when did you realize you brought peace to others?

_____

_____

_____

_____

_____

_____

_____

_____

_____

_____

_____

DAY 5

"An ill-tempered man stirs up strife, but a patient man allays discord."
(Proverbs 15:18)

For years I had worked in the corporate sector and wondered what could turn a nice, sweet person into a raging drama-queen (or king). I have seen it over and over in my professional career. A "good" employee who was always happy started spending more time with an ill-tempered person. Within two months, the "good" employee's behavior changed. The once-happy, hard-working employee was now angry, jealous, and non-responsive.

Attitude and behaviors are contagious. After years of witnessing these cases, it became clear how easily we are influenced by the people in our lives. We have people who enjoy causing strife just because they can. They enjoy the chaos, the messiness that comes with stirring up trouble. They get everyone worked up and then sit back to enjoy the show. In other words, hurt people hurt others. They are probably in a place of pain, but instead of working on themselves, they create more pain.

The good news, my friends, is you don't have to fall prey to their games. You can be cordial and respectful to everyone around you but still keep your distance. Your future demands a calm, patient mind. Your time is too precious to waste playing games that won't lead you to your higher self.

Reflection Time:

Do you know any drama queens/kings? Have you even been drawn into their games but didn't understand how it happened? This is a great time to stop listening to the people in your life who enjoy causing strife and find ways to minimize your exposure to them. You don't have to avoid them but less time with them could be very beneficial.

_____
_____
_____
_____
_____
_____
_____
_____
_____
_____
_____
_____

DAY 6

"The patient man shows much good sense, but the quick-tempered man displays folly at its height."
(Proverbs 14:29)

As you probably realized, a very common theme in the scriptures mentioned is patience. They remind us over and over not to be too quick to react and to keep our tempers under control. If you're wondering why, it's because our initial reactions usually lead to rash decisions. If we are always reacting with our feelings at the slightest provocation, our reactions will be careless and overboard.

Every battle is not worth fighting. Taking our time to analyze a situation gives us space to calm down and look at things from a fresh perspective. In doing this, we ensure that we don't become victims of our tempers. Instead, we need to maintain our surrounding peaceful. Sometimes it's easier to ask for clarification on what the other person means before jumping to conclusions about their intentions. Many fights can be avoided if we come from a place of understanding instead of judgement.

Patience will give us peace of mind and provide us with a barrier from making impulsive decisions. It allows us to have time to respond to things. Nothing is forcing us to react to everything that comes our way immediately or allowing our tempers to rule us.

Reflection Time:

Do you consider yourself a patient person? If not, what is holding you back from being one? If you are a patient person, are you more patient with others or with yourself? Can you improve how patient you are with yourself?

_____

_____

_____

_____

_____

_____

_____

_____

_____

_____

_____

_____

DAY 7

"Merciful and gracious is the Lord, slow to anger, abounding in kindness."
(Psalms 103:8)

We are coming to the end of week one, and the question we're now facing is: how are we to face our anger? The Psalm above gives us a beautiful solution. It states we should be slow to anger while having an abundance of kindness. We have seen people in our lives who rarely get mad. They have this internal joy in their soul and just radiate youth (regardless of their age).

My father is that way. In his seventies, he looks and acts like he has barely hit fifty. He is the picture of joy. He has shared his secret with me, so now I will share it with you: he conquered his temper early in his life and became more patient. According to my father, he was quick to anger and threw tantrums when things didn't go his way. This is hard to image now since it takes a great deal of things going on for my father to get mad. He is always working on trying to see the other person's point of view and accept others as they are. My father is a magnet for people to gravitate toward because he makes those around him feel safe and at ease.

Like my father, we all have choices we can make. We can give up and just resign ourselves to be ill-tempered and easy to anger. Or we can decide to keep strife out of our lives and change our mindset. It's all a personal decision and nobody else can do it for us. If we want a life rich with joy and peace, then we must choose to have it.

Reflection Time:

If impatience, ill-temperedness, and fits of anger are things plaguing you, write down five things showing how these things have helped you in your life. If you're not able to find reasons why keeping these feelings and behaviors around are serving you, then it's time to let them go. Things that aren't taking you to a higher level aren't worth keeping around.

_____

_____

_____

_____

_____

_____

_____

_____

_____

_____

_____

CONGRATULATIONS MY FRIEND!

You have completed your first week in this devotional. We live in very demanding times, with things always fighting for our attention. I'm excited you made this agreement with yourself to stick with this devotional and give yourself time to look deep in your soul. Forgiveness is not something we talk much about, but not addressing it can have very negative consequences.

As we saw this week, being quick to anger or having an ill-temper are things that can hold us back in our path to growth and happiness. The scriptures urge us to be patient. To work at being kind-hearted and not give into our feelings. Paying people back for offenses they have committed against us only continues to feed the fire of anger. The more time we dwell on those negative thoughts, the bigger the situation becomes in our minds.

The good news, my friends, is we have a choice. We get to choose if we want to be patient or not. The power is within us to decide how we want to react to the things that come against us. Trust me, my friends, I'm not saying this process is easy, but it is possible. It is possible to have peace in our days and still be passionate about our dreams. As we continue this devotional, please relax and give yourself permission to be okay right now. Remember that life is a journey, and our goal is to grow each day.

Week 1 –

Reflection Time:

As we wrap up Week One, take a couple of minutes to reflect on any thoughts, emotions, or patterns that arose during your journey. Did anything jump out at you during this week that you weren't aware you were holding on to? Are you seeing yourself in a different light? What thoughts, feelings, or emotions are you still holding inside that aren't serving you anymore?

_____

_____

_____

_____

_____

_____

_____

_____

_____

_____

_____

WEEK 2

FORGIVING OTHERS

In our current society, they teach us to believe that it's not okay to be vulnerable. We don't want to be perceived as weak or allow people to "walk" all over us. When transgressions are committed against us, our first reaction is to pay people back. But as we explored in week one, hurt people hurt others.

Forgiveness is not a simple thing to do or practice. It's easier to hold on to an offense. Our self-defense mechanism kicks in and reminds us constantly that we were hurt, and we shouldn't trust others. The problem with this mindset is that it constricts the way we see the world and poisons our soul. We judge others for the things they do and fill our hearts with bitterness and disappointment.

The pain, suffering, mistrust, and anger we hold in our heart for the actions of others are all emotions we drag around with us like suitcases. It's very hard to pick up joy, peace, and happiness if you're already full because you're carrying all these negative emotions with you. We forgive others, not for their sake but for ours. Forgiveness does not make us weak. Quite the contrary. It gives us control of our lives. We take back the power to stop the suffering and move on to a greater future.

DAY 8

"When his brothers saw that their father loved him best of all his sons, they hated him so much that they would not even greet him."
(Genesis 37:4)

Some of the most common questions I get asked when the topic of forgiveness is brought up are: How do I forgive when I was hurt? How can I let go when I was betrayed? Why should I forgive people when they took everything from me? If anyone can relate to those questions, it would be Joseph. Joseph was one of the youngest sons of Jacob. He was hated, envied, and despised by his brothers because his father loved him the best.

Joseph never asked to be the favorite. He was just doing his best, loving his family and honoring his father. Unfortunately, the envy of his brothers went so deep that they conspired to kill Joseph. At the last minute, instead of killing him, they sold him as a slave to a passing caravan. Hate and anger can make people do horrible things, even to their own family.

Joseph had many reasons to become hateful. Instead, he kept doing his best as he faced mistreatment and adversaries. The Lord blessed his sacrifices by making him second in command over Egypt. Joseph had the opportunity to pay his brothers back when they arrived at the palace asking for help. What Joseph did next was amazing. He forgave his brothers and even fed them. Like Joseph, we will have decisions to make to either hold onto grudges or forgive those who wronged us. The life we live will be determined by the decisions we make.

Reflection Time:

Do you have people in your life who have done you wrong? Can you forgive the harm they have done to you, even if you never speak to them again? Or are the wounds so deep that you cannot forgive them?

_____

_____

_____

_____

_____

_____

_____

_____

_____

_____

_____

_____

DAY 9

"Because of their wicked avarice I was angry, and struck them, hiding myself in wrath, as they went their own rebellious ways." (Isaiah 57:17)

Honestly, my friends, some of us are not as godly as Joseph. He was one of the great heroes of faith, and his compassion had no end. At times we are more like Isaiah in the scripture above. We become enraged by what others have done to us and we retaliate. We take vengeance against our trespassers. The problem that arises from this is we are left with the anger and wrath and it eats at our souls.

Those who offended us have no issues moving on with their lives and not thinking of the pain they've caused. They aren't sitting around worrying about our struggles or suffering. We're the ones holding onto the offense, the anger, and the pain. We are the ones putting our lives on hold, doubting ourselves while convincing ourselves that the world is out to get us.

Forgiving those who offend us releases us from that all-consuming wrath that takes over. It gives us an opportunity to face those who hurt us without hate or shame. But forgiveness means not thinking about the situation anymore. It means not plotting about how to get revenge, and it means not bringing on another altercation. They aren't just words, but actions we take for letting go and separating ourselves from the past and moving on.

Reflection Time:

Do you have a situation you're holding on to because the pain is too great to let go? Was the person who hurt you close to you? Are you willing to forgive them knowing this will bring healing to your life?

_____

_____

_____

_____

_____

_____

_____

_____

_____

_____

_____

_____

_____

DAY 10

"You see for yourself today that the Lord just now delivered you into my grasp in the cave. I had some thought of killing you, but I took pity on you instead." (1 Samuel 24:11)

The stories of King David are legendary. From the time he was a boy and killed the giant Goliath, to the king he became and loved God beyond words. His actions are carefully documented in the bible. What we don't hear a lot about are the struggles he experienced before becoming king. They anointed him to be king and to replace the ruling monarch Saul.

When David was a young man, King Saul loved him. As David grew, his fame surpassed that of the king. Saul become jealous and was full of poison toward the young man. The king spent years chasing David and his men through the wilderness trying to kill him. There is nothing in the scriptures that shows that David ever did anything wrong against Saul to merit his rage. David was just following the will of the Lord, yet he was hunted, tormented, and mistreated.

He had the opportunity to pay Saul back as the scripture above shows us. Instead of ending the king's life, he spared him. When the opportunity comes to pay back someone who has done us wrong, what would we do? Can we be like David and forgive them, spare them, and move on with our lives? This is the decision we will eventually have to make. To achieve our next level in life, we must be comfortable with forgiving others even when they don't deserve it.

Reflection Time:

Have you even been distracted or taken off course by trying to pay someone back? How much energy do you spend on this journey? Looking back now, what other things could you have accomplished if you weren't distracted with that mission?

_____

_____

_____

_____

_____

_____

_____

_____

_____

_____

_____

_____

DAY 11

*"But I say to you, whoever is angry with his brother will be liable
to judgement, and whoever says to his brother, 'Raqa,' will be answerable
to the Sanhedrin, and whoever says, 'You fool,' will be liable to fiery
Gehenna.." (Matthew 5:22)*

Holding resentment toward others was something that Jesus took seriously. Jesus explained how the anger you felt toward your brother would eventually come back against you. As the anger escalated, so would the punishment. Eventually, the person who was angry toward his brother would end up burning for all eternity.

Why would being angry toward others be such a big deal? We all get angry. We are all emotional beings, and anger is a natural emotion. What we do with this anger is where things can become tricky. Uncontrollable anger and hate, as the scripture explained, can lead to murder. Your reaction to an offense can be just as bad, if not worse, than the offense itself.

This might seem extreme at first but look at all the cases in the news of homicides that are described as crimes of passion. During an uncontrollable spell of rage, people have killed others. Letting go of anger and forgiving people as quickly as possible releases us from its grip and gives us room to think properly.

Reflection Time:

Have you ever found yourself upset or angry with someone for more than a day? Did the other person know they had offended you? Did you share your feelings with them? Were you able to forgive them?

_____

_____

_____

_____

_____

_____

_____

_____

_____

_____

DAY 12

"Where do the wars and where do the conflicts among you come from? Is it not from your passions that make war within your members?"
(James 4:1)

If anger can lead to murder, then the idea of war and conflict can easily be understood. Our conflicts and dissatisfactions can be traced back to minor transgressions that escalated out of control. Things like jealousy, anger, fear, and discontent can all lead people to hate others. One person wants something they think the other person doesn't deserve. An act is committed, and the other person retaliates. The cycle continues unless people make a conscious choice to stop it. Anger can easily take root in our hearts when we focus on the offenses against us.

Hate and anger not only poison our soul, they also steal valuable time that we need to reach our destiny. We become distracted in battles we were not meant to fight by trying to pay people back. The consuming desire of being right has a certain level of appeal. We fall prey to it, so in turn we lose sight of the big picture.

Disagreements usually start with small things. By forgiving people, we can focus on our future. They don't drag us into conflict that wouldn't end well. Just because a person wants to argue with you doesn't mean you need to engage. You can keep your peace and avoid altercations by paying attention to how you react to others and not falling into their trap. Your destiny is waiting.

Reflection Time:

When was the last time you walked away from an argument? Were you able to keep your focus and avoid engaging with the other person? Did you notice how you felt when you didn't argue with the other person?

_____

_____

_____

_____

_____

_____

_____

_____

_____

_____

_____

DAY 13

"If your brother sins, rebuke him; and if he repents, forgive him.
And if he wrongs you seven times in one day and returns to you seven
times saying, 'I am sorry,' you should forgive him."
(Luke 17:3-4)

I have witnessed many discussions on interpreting Christ's words when it comes to forgiveness. The main question people ask is this: How many times should we forgive a person? Some scriptures say seventy-seven. Others, like the one we are focusing on today, say seven. Regardless of the number, the meaning stays the same. We should forgive as many times as a person asks for forgiveness.

This is a hard concept for us to follow. We spend a lot of time trying to understand the intentions of the person before we give our forgiveness. Here is the part in Luke's scripture that gives us more clarity. If someone hurts us, we should confront them. It allows us to speak our truth. We are allowed to tell the other person how their actions made us feel. Once we have addressed the situation, if they repent, then we should forgive. It is not up to us to pass judgment on others, but we may share how a comment or action affects us.

There is power when we express our feelings. We can communicate our emotions and not allow them to boil inside of us. The repression of those feelings can be just as toxic as not forgiving.

Reflection Time:

How many times have you forgiven the same person? Has it been for the same offense or different ones? Do you believe they are sorry and didn't mean to hurt you? If not, why are you still associating with that person? Can you break the cycle and stay away from them?

DAY 14

"We urge you, brothers, admonish the idle, cheer the fainthearted, support the weak, be patient with all. See that no one returns evil for evil; rather, always seek what is good [both] for each other and for all."
(1 Thessalonians 5:14-15)

Over the last week we have spoken a lot about the importance of forgiveness. Yesterday, we learned that we should rebuke people who have sinned against us. The key for this week, like in week one, comes back to being patient. Patience with ourselves to not jump to conclusions and become upset with others when they do things we don't approve of. Patience with others who are also working on their own personal growth and process.

We can't make assumptions on the intentions of others. We don't know why they do certain things and what motivates them. Sometimes disputes are a series of miscommunications that could have been avoided by trying to listen to the other person. We have the power to treat people with respect while not reacting to the way they treat us.

As we get ready to wrap up week two, please remember this: do not return evil with evil. We will encounter hateful people in our lives. Don't join that crowd. You have a choice on how you live every day. Evil will only produce more evil. Forgiveness of others frees us from those chains of suffering. You are not a slave to your temper. Nobody can take your peace unless you let them.

Reflection Time:

Are you willing to forgive the transgressions that were done to you? Are you ready to forgive and let go? If not, what is holding you back from taking this leap of faith?

_____

_____

_____

_____

_____

_____

_____

_____

_____

_____

_____

CONGRATULATIONS MY FRIEND!

You have completed Week Two in this devotional. I'm thrilled to be with you on this journey. If you're ready to forgive those people that hurt you, you have several ways you can do it. One, you can approach the person directly. You can set up a meeting with them to discuss your feelings in a secure environment. There is no yelling or screaming, just a discussion of how their actions hurt you, but you're moving on.

Second, if the person is not around or the conversation is not possible, you can still forgive them in your heart. You can accomplish this by writing a letter to the person expressing how their actions made you feel. The letter doesn't have to be mailed. You can burn it, bury it, or destroy it. The goal is to release the pain and suffering from your soul. You can perform this exercise as many times as you need to get to your ultimate goal: forgiveness.

Forgiveness becomes easier with practice. This doesn't make us weak. On the contrary, it gives us the power to live up to our highest potential. Our soul is not contaminated with hate and anger. We have space to fill it with love, joy, and dreams of a better future.

DARE TO FORGIVE

Week 2 –

Reflection Time:

We have completed Week Two together, my friends. Let's take a couple of minutes to reflect on any ideas, emotions, or random thoughts that have popped up during the week. Write anything that caught you by surprise and anything that caused you a moment of pause. As we discuss the power of forgiving others, make a list of the people you should forgive to clear the emotional space in your heart.

_____

_____

_____

_____

_____

_____

_____

_____

_____

_____

_____

_____

WEEK 3

FORGIVING OURSELVES

We are halfway through this devotional. I hope you are seeing the importance of forgiveness in your lives. Sometimes it's easier to forgive the actions of others than it is to forgive ourselves. We have all heard the saying: We are our own worst enemies. We have a tendency to talk to ourselves more negatively than we do others. At times, we hurt ourselves more than any other person ever would.

Forgiveness, like charity, must start at home. For us, this means forgiveness must start in our souls. We must be willing to see ourselves as worthy of forgiveness. That our sins, transgressions, and failures deserve to be forgiven like any other persons. Nothing we have done in our lives deserves a lifetime of suffering and torture. Our justice system is designed for people to pay for their crimes once. After that sentence is met, they are released back into society. Forgiveness of ourselves has the same result, if we accept it.

We must see ourselves with the same love and compassion the Lord sees in us. To believe we are worthy of his love and that he has forgiven us already. Once we believe this, we can start letting go of our own self-hate and anger. Just like anger toward others eat at our souls, that anger will destroy us if it is directed toward ourselves. Be kind to yourself, my friends, during this week, and know that you are loved and cared for. You deserve to live a life of peace and compassion.

DAY 15

"The Lord said to Samuel: 'How long will you grieve for Saul, whom I rejected as king of Israel? Fill your horn with oil, and be on your way.'" (1 Samuel 16:1)

Most people hold themselves to a different standard than they do other people. We are more critical of ourselves and hold onto things for longer periods of time. Samuel is a splendid example of this. He had anointed Saul to be the first king of Israel, but Saul failed at following the will of the Lord. Samuel took Saul's failure as a personal reflection of himself. Instead of letting it go, he grieved and fell apart.

Saul's indiscretion had nothing to do with Samuel. Samuel did everything in his power to advise Saul and give him direction, yet Saul did his own thing. Saul was not interested in following the path the Lord had set for him. This lack of character was something Samuel took personal. Saul's actions overwhelmed him with shame and grief.

It took the Lord to remind Samuel to let it go. He had anointed Saul, sure, but that didn't make Saul his responsibility. Taking someone's mistakes and failures as our own isn't heathy, even if the person is a child or a spouse. Forgive them for their actions, but also forgive yourself for whatever pain they caused. Let go of carrying other people's crosses. You have your own life to live, and you cannot do it while suffering for others.

Reflection Time:

Have you been feeling ashamed or overwhelmed for the actions of people in your life? Have you, like Samuel, taken ownership of the things others have done because you're close to that person? If so, write five things you can do to forgive that person and yourself.

_____

_____

_____

_____

_____

_____

_____

_____

_____

_____

_____

_____

DAY 16

"All day long my disgrace is before me; shame has covered my face. At the sound of those who taunt me and revile, at the sight of the spiteful enemy." (Psalms 44:16-17)

Disgrace and shame are a very dangerous combination. Judging ourselves through the glasses of shame make everything we do seem insignificant, like nothing is ever enough. We undermine our accomplishments and are even embarrassed for our success because of our own disgrace. We make decisions assuming the world is judging us in the same way we are judging ourselves.

This view we have of ourselves will become self-sabotaging. We pass on opportunities because we don't believe we deserve them. We avoid taking chances because of the way we see our own image. My friends, let me tell you this: you have done nothing so despicable that forgiveness is beyond your reach. Regardless of what people say. What you say about yourself is the most important thing.

Forgiveness is your birth right, and the Lord gives it freely. It's your job to take it and forgive yourself. To embrace forgiveness and let go of the disgrace and shame that hold you back. You may hold your head up high, unlike the Psalms who wanted to cover his face. You deserve peace and happiness, so start by accepting it.

Reflection Time:

Take a few moments, my friends, to write all the things you feel ashamed of. Make a list, and then ask yourself if this was a friend asking you to forgive them, would you refuse? To forgive ourselves, we must first see ourselves as our own best friend. A person in need of healing and who is remorseful. If we are willing to forgive others, then we must extend the same compassion toward ourselves.

_____

_____

_____

_____

_____

_____

_____

_____

_____

_____

_____

DAY 17

"By these you too once conducted yourselves, when you lived in that way. But now you must put them all away: anger, fury, malice, slander, and obscene language out of your mouths." (Colossians 3:7-8)

Knowing the context in which the bible was written makes an enormous difference in understanding what the scriptures are trying to convey. It wasn't until later in life that I learned the letters in the New Testament written by Paul were directed to newly converted Christians. I had never taken the time to study the origin of the scriptures, but merely read or heard the passages from different books. The background changed my perspective. Paul wasn't talking to "holy" people who did everything perfect. He was talking to people like me who were searching for a better way to live and heal.

Paul reminds the Colossians in this scripture that their lives had changed. Before they were introduced to Christ, they were full of anger, fury, and the likes. But now they knew better. The people needed to make a personal decision to change their ways. Change starts from within. Before we can give forgiveness to others, it must first live in our hearts. We can't feel love in our heart if we're full of anger. We can't feel compassion if malice is brewing in our soul.

To truly forgive those around us, we must first forgive ourselves. A simple way to start is to remind ourselves what Paul says: we didn't know any better before. We were doing the best we could with the information we had at the time. We can now make conscious changes. By investing in ourselves, we can be gentle with our growing process and start healing.

Reflection Time:

Are there some areas in your life you would like to change? Do you have habits that are holding you back from living your best life now and forgiving yourself?

_____

_____

_____

_____

_____

_____

_____

_____

_____

_____

_____

DAY 18

"You have been snared by the utterance of your lips,
caught by the words of your mouth;
So do this, my son, to free yourself, since you have fallen into your
neighbor's power." (Proverbs 6:2-3)

We are in the middle of week three and this is all about how to forgive ourselves. This Proverb is very interesting. It describes one of the things that are holding us back are the words coming out of our mouths. Yes, many of us spend a lot of time talking about other people. Unfortunately, some of us have lived a lifetime of putting ourselves down. We have mastered the art of critiquing and attacking everything we do and the dreams we have.

Our words have power, and they can be weapons of mass destruction. Especially when they are directed toward us. The words our subconscious hears over and over have a way of taking root in our minds and becoming self-fulfilling prophecies. We fall victim to the mindset of not being good enough. We create a place where we torture ourselves for the same mistakes over and over.

The good news is we can break the cycle. Just like the justice system releases prisoners, it is time to pardon yourself from your faults and transgressions. Now is the time to change the words you tell yourself. You have the power to bless yourself like you have the power to curse yourself. Stop the vicious process of self-judgement and hate. Give yourself permission to be free of pain.

Reflection Time:

Today, take a few minutes to create an affirmation list. Each statement should start with "I am." Even if you don't feel like the things on your list, by writing them down and repeating them to yourself every day, you will start to reprogram your mind. Affirmation statements are powerful since they're going directly into your subconscious mind. Here are a few to get you started:

I am talented.
I am beautiful.
I am loving.
I am forgiving.
I am creative.

_____

_____

_____

_____

_____

_____

_____

_____

_____

_____

_____

_____

DAY 19

*"Insult has broken my heart, and I am weak; I looked for
compassion, but there was none, for comforters, but found none."*
(Psalms 69:21)

How often have you felt broken and weak? After my
divorce, this was a very common feeling for me. I was sure I
was being judged by everyone who saw me. In the back of
my mind, I felt that my faults and failures defined my entire
life. I was looking for someone around me to help me heal. I
didn't realize strength came from within. Like David in this
Psalm, I was looking for compassion and comfort from
external sources.

In my search, I kept looking for validation that I was
still a good person. The problem was, I didn't believe I
deserved it. I had fallen into a vicious cycle of self-sabotage
and self-pity. While I wanted people to give me compassion
and love, I didn't think I was good enough to receive it. I
hadn't forgiven myself for the pain I had caused, so I
couldn't believe the compassion of others.

If you're stuck in a place like I was, where people are
offering you support but you won't accept it, stop. Please let
these words reach into your soul. You are valuable. You are
powerful, and you deserve to live a life full of joy and love.
That guilt you're carrying is not serving you anymore. To
have a better future, you need to stop carrying the past with
you.

Reflection Time:

Take a few moments to reflect on your life. Do you have any guilt you're carrying? Are you holding onto your past because you feel you don't deserve to be happy? Only by acknowledging that you're carrying these things can you start the healing process.

_____

_____

_____

_____

_____

_____

_____

_____

_____

_____

_____

_____

DAY 20

"By your stubbornness and impenitent heart, you are storing up wrath for yourself for the day of wrath and revelation of the just judgment of God, who will repay everyone according to his works." (Romans 2:5-6)

Today's scripture is very interesting. It reminds us that we are the ones who choose to hold onto things, to store wrath in our souls. We are the ones, by our stubbornness, who do not let go of old grudges. The Lord has a plan for each one of us. He wants us to be happy and live a blessed live. When we ask for forgiveness, he grants it immediately. The Lord is not holding onto his blessings and mercy to make us suffer. The scripture reminds us that we are the ones trying to carry out the judgement of God, not just sitting back and expecting God to take care of it.

If the Lord wants to bless us, why are we still holding onto self-hate, self-doubt, and this feeling of worthlessness? What is making us stubborn in this area of healing? It's probably the fact that it feels good to validate our insecurities. It takes away the responsibility of moving forward. We can fall back on old habits of not being good enough and tell ourselves that we don't deserve good things. This is a victim mindset, my friends. Forgiveness helps us break from those shackles.

The Lord forgives all of our transgressions. Now believe it and move forward toward your future. Allow yourself to be free of shame, guilt, and self-doubt. Know that you are loved and that the Almighty wants you to have all the blessings of this world.

Reflection Time:

Today, my friends, I urge you to make a commitment with yourself to be gentle in your growth process. Take a few minutes to write a letter to yourself expressing your love and how proud you are of the progress you have made. Give yourself thanks for being willing to change and be grateful for all the good things to come.

_____

_____

_____

_____

_____

_____

_____

_____

_____

_____

_____

CONGRATULATIONS MY FRIENDS!

We have completed our third week together and it has been one incredible journey. This week has been all about our own self-healing. It takes courage to change, to face our guilt and shame. The process of letting go of years of programing and believing the self-limiting beliefs that we don't deserve to be forgiven is not a simple one. It takes time to reprogram ourselves to believe we are worthy of compassion and love.

While healing can be challenging, the results are incredible. We can see ourselves in a new light. To believe that our dreams can come true because we are worthy of them. By healing ourselves, we can be more understanding of others instead of using our hurt to hurt them. Healing comes with time and patience, but we have to be willing to do the work. Remember my friends, your future is worth it.

Take a leap of faith. If you haven't started your healing journey, please start. Time is precious and you can't spend another moment torturing yourself with guilt and shame. It's time to liberate yourself from those shackles and enjoy the life the Lord wants for you.

Week 3 –

Reflection Time:

As we wrap up Week Three, take a few moments to explore your thoughts and feelings from this week. Write anything that you noticed during your reflection times. Spend some time considering how your feelings and thoughts have changed regarding self-forgiveness and think about some tools you found that can help you deal with those things. Remember to be gentle with yourself. This process takes time. If you feel the pain is too overwhelming, don't be afraid to ask for help from a trusted friend, a religious leader, or a medical professional. This process doesn't have to be done alone.

_____

_____

_____

_____

_____

_____

_____

_____

_____

_____

_____

_____

D. C. GOMEZ

WEEK 4

LIVING IN PEACE

We are living in a time of turmoil and uncertainty. It's hard to imagine a life of peace and happiness. But what if I told you that is exactly the life you could live right now? The outside world doesn't have to affect your inner state of being. You can be part of the world without the world being inside of you. This state occurs when your mind and soul are at ease, and the stresses of the world don't disturb you.

How do we achieve this state? By not harboring ill feelings toward others. By willing to forgive as quickly as an offense takes place and not holding grudges. A state of peace and joy comes when our minds are not fighting a constant battle between what we want and what we think we deserve. Self-forgiveness and forgiving others are essential to find peace in our day and in our homes.

As we embark on this week together, we will look over some things we covered in the past three weeks. We will remind ourselves of the life the Lord wants for us and how that life is closer than we think. Remember, we are worthy of the blessings the Lord has for us. We just need to believe we deserve them.

DAY 22

"The quick-tempered man makes a fool of himself, but the prudent man is at peace." (Proverbs 14-17)

I usually joke with people that I have a very boring life. I write a lot of drama in my fictional books, but my actual life is very low key. I make it a point to have a drama-free life and as much peace as possible. I learned the hard way that I was inefficient when my life was in chaos and full of turmoil (probably like many people). One thing that helped me clear some of the drama out of my life was not holding onto offenses and grudges. I stopped keeping up with the actions of others.

The Proverbs above helps to clarify this point. We all have options in our lives. We can jump to conclusions, be offended, and seek retaliation. Our current society encourages us to be right and win. But that also brings fights, hate, and extra stress nobody really needs. We can't reach our true potential if we're wasting time fighting battles that aren't meant to be fought. Be slow to anger, my friends.

How do we change if we have a quick temper? By becoming intentional in our actions and thoughts. Before we take action, step away from the situation. We can't control the things that happened, but we can control how we react to them. We can take our time to answer to an offense by asking ourselves one question: Will this still matter in five years? If the answer is no, we can let it go and move on. Our peace is worth more than winning a fight.

Reflection Time:

Are you living in a peaceful environment, or are you stressed and full of worries? If you are finding yourself overwhelmed and frustrated, what are some things that are plaguing your mind. Take a few minutes to write them down.

_____

_____

_____

_____

_____

_____

_____

_____

_____

_____

_____

_____

DAY 23

"Do to other as you would have then do to you. Love your enemies and do good them, and lend expecting nothing back; then your reward will be great and you will be children of the Most High, for he himself is kind to the ungrateful and the wicked."
(Luke 6:31,35)

It's easy to do "good" to those who have been good to us or people we love. It's difficult to be kind to those who have done us harm. My mother has a saying, "Never deny help to those who need it, even if they don't deserve it." As a child, those things were very hard to understand. Why should I help people who didn't like me or mistreated me? But my mother would model this principle over and over by helping people who had been hateful toward her without a second thought.

As an adult, I've learned we help others for our own peace, not for the actions of the other person. We help not because we expect them to say thank you, but because goodness is contagious. I am a true believer that acts of kindness will change the world. We never know who is watching our actions and how a minor act toward someone could inspire other in their own lives.

By having a giving soul, resentment can't take root. Our first thoughts are not of mistrust but joy toward the surrounding things. We see the world with kindness and hope instead of bitterness and anger. This change in mindset has a ripple effect in our lives, and it helps us to be more kind and patient with ourselves.

Reflection Time:

Write all the acts of kindness you have done in the last six months. If you haven't been able to do many, don't worry. Instead, write the things you would like to do for others in the upcoming months. What are some things you can do for the people around you that would help them out and that they aren't expecting?

_____

_____

_____

_____

_____

_____

_____

_____

_____

_____

_____

_____

_____

DAY 24

"Be not friendly with hotheaded man, nor the companion of a wrathful man, Lest you learn his ways, and get yourself into a snare."
(Proverbs 22:24-25)

Just like acts of kindness are contagious, so are negative behaviors. Some of us are more prone at picking up other people's influences and energies than others. I'm one of those people who can easily pick up the mood of others if I'm not careful. If I spend a lot of time with angry and paranoid individuals, within a few weeks I will start acting the same way. Minor offenses that I normally will ignore will seem like a personal attack deserving of retaliation.

By now you're probably aware that I enjoy my calm, "boring" life. I enjoy having peaceful days without worrying about who is talking about me. To have this peace, I had to be intentional with the people I associated with. Don't get me wrong, I didn't make an announcement to the world telling them I am distancing myself from people. I just became more conscious of the time I was spending with people who were negative and reduced the amount.

The best way to live a life where we can forgive easily is to not hold grudges. If the company we keep is always looking for offenses and disagreements, we will eventually do the same. We must guard our space, my friends. Peace and joy are the ways for a prosperous life, but this is something we must work on.

Reflection Time:

Do you have people in your life who are always negative and criticize everyone? Is it possible for you to minimize the time you spend with them? If this is not the case, you'll need to stay on guard to spot how their moods and behaviors affect you. Find ways to balance their influence with positive energy in your own life.

DAY 25

"Do not be conquered by evil but conquer evil with good."
(Romans 12-21)

Conquering evil with good is a common theme throughout the New Testament. It's an empowering message that we are not victims but conquerors. That as a race—the human-race—we have options about how we carry ourselves in our lives. We get to choose how we battle every situation and how we handle the offenses in our lives. Choosing forgiveness and love is not always the most popular choice in current times. People want to be offended and prove their point. But that doesn't create unity around us or bring peace to our lives.

The choice is always ours. And so are the consequences that come with our choices. A heart full of hate and discontent for itself and others will eventually rot. That hate that is inside will manifest on the surface of the body. We all know people who are angry and grouchy all the time. They physically look mean and old and worn out. Our bodies are a reflection of our soul. Those emotions have a way of coming to the surface and taking a toll, even in our looks.

Now think of someone you know who is older but is full of joy. Their personality shines through, making them appear younger. Avoid evil thoughts, my friends, for a healthy and happy life. Let your joy shine through and your body will reflect it.

Reflection Time:

Take a couple of minutes to reflect on the people in your life who are always happy and full of joy. What are some things they have in common? Study some of their characteristics and things you admire about them.

_____

_____

_____

_____

_____

_____

_____

_____

_____

_____

_____

DAY 26

"He who pursues justice and kindness will find life and honor."
(Proverbs 21:21)

Proverbs is one of my favorite books in the bible. It is filled with practical, timeless advice that we can all implement. The scripture above falls perfectly into our week. We all want a long life that is blessed with prosperity and joy. To get this life, even in the Old Testament, their answer was the same: be kind to others and treat people with respect. This is nothing new. On the contrary, it's a basic principle we teach most kids.

Notice that it says nothing about being just if others are good to us. Or to only be kind toward "nice" people. It states if we pursue a life full of justice and are kind toward everyone we encounter, our rewards will be great. We are asked to do good expecting nothing back. To not have wrath or anger in our hearts and to give without conditions. To be people full of joy just because we're giving the gift of life.

This might sound like an impossible task. We live in a world full of people, and some are not nice. That is true. But we are only responsible for ourselves. We are not responsible for paying people back, but for focusing on our own happiness and growth. Remember, you can only control your reaction to others. Give the rest to the Lord.

Reflection Time:

How can you show your love for the people around you? Who are the people that support you no matter what? This doesn't require buying things for people. It might be as simple as a text or a call to tell them you're thinking about them. Spreading joy is as simple as a smile, and all it takes is a minor act of kindness.

_____

_____

_____

_____

_____

_____

_____

_____

_____

_____

_____

DAY 27

"Only goodness and love will pursue me all the days of my life."
(Psalm 23-6)

Every time I read this scripture I can't help but smile. Many people are familiar with Psalm Twenty-Three. The beginning of the Psalm starts with, "As I walk through the valley of the Shadow of Death, I will fear no evil." That is a powerful statement. In this Psalm, King David expresses his trust in the Lord regardless of the situation he is facing. The scripture above is just as powerful, but not as famous. David gives us a beautiful promise to hold on to.

Can you imagine a life where only "goodness and love" are chasing us? This is the promise the Lord has for us. But we have to believe we deserve this. We first must forgive that inner child inside of us for all the offenses we keep tracking. We must forgive the transgressions done against us and empty our soul of hate and malice. Only when our souls are empty of this poison can love and goodness pour in.

There is always good news when it comes to the Lord. We can choose to forgive. This is a conscious decision we all can make. We have control if we want to heal and move on with our lives. But we must take the first steps. Only when we choose to forgive will peace follow us.

Reflection Time:

Have you taken the leap of faith and forgiven yourself and others? If not, take a few minutes to write down what is holding you back.

_____

_____

_____

_____

_____

_____

_____

_____

_____

_____

_____

_____

_____

DAY 28

"With closest custody, guard your heart, for in it are the sources of life." *(Proverbs 4:23)*

This is a powerful scripture to finish our fourth week together. The true source of our life and happiness lies in our hearts. We must be vigilant to guard it against hate, anger, resentment, and negative thoughts. The field of our souls is rich, and whatever we let take root in it will grow. We can have a harvest of joy, love, and peace, or we can have a harvest of bitterness, cynicism, and discontent.

We are the ones that water those seeds. The feelings we hold toward others don't affect those people, but they do affect us. Those emotions have a way of shaping everything we do and say. The life we want is within our grasp if we are willing to get it. The key is to be on guard and intentional with the people we associate with and guard the information that comes our way.

We are meant to live a happy, fulfilled life. But if we're trying to pay people back, we will never experience it. We cannot live our best life now if we're holding ourselves back because of previous shame. I challenge you, my friends, to forgive and to let the goodness of the Lord into your heart.

Reflection Time:

Are you willing to guard your heart and protect your dreams? What are some things you can do to keep negative thoughts at bay and stay focused on your dreams and goals?

_____

_____

_____

_____

_____

_____

_____

_____

_____

_____

_____

CONGRATULATIONS MY FRIENDS!

We have completed our fourth week in this devotional and have come to the end of our journey together. I pray this journey has been as fulfilling and empowering for you as it was for me. During our weeks together, we focused on the need to forgive not only others but ourselves. The process of self-healing can be challenging, but if you're feeling stuck in your life, you already know it's necessary.

Always remember, my friends, that you are blessed and highly favored. The Lord wants you to have an incredible future full of joy and peace. The first step is to heal and let go of the things that are holding you back. You are not alone in this journey. He walks with you always. The Lord understands our struggles like no one else can.

Thank you for allowing me to be a part of this journey with you and welcoming me into your home. It has truly been an honor to spend these four weeks with you. I believe in your future and the blessing you bring to the world.

If you would like to continue this journey together, I recommend getting a copy of *Dare to Love,* the next installment in the Dare Collection.

Week 4 –

Reflection time:

This last reflection is an open one, an opportunity for you to write anything that comes to your mind. Any ideas, questions, or thoughts that come to mind that you would like to explore in-depth, or just a safe space to dream again. Forgiveness is your birthright, my friends. Never doubt that.

_____

_____

_____

_____

_____

_____

_____

_____

_____

_____

_____

_____

ACKNOWLEDGEMENTS

I'm a believer that it truly takes a village to bring a book to life. I'm blessed by the incredible and talented people the Lord has put in my life as part of my village.

This devotional would not have been possible without the incredible Ms. Cassandra Fear. Not only is she an incredible writer, she is an amazing editor and cover designer. Thank you so much, sweetie, for both editing and creating the cover for this book.

My deepest thanks go to the talented Ms. Courtney Shockey for making my words look amazing on the page. Her patience with me is always incredible.

Thank you to my family for always believing in my dreams, even when they always seem too far to reach.

Above all, my love and thanks go to you, my dear friends. Thank you for allowing me to be a part of this journey with you. I believe in you and I believe that you are destined for amazing things.